ARIES

HOROSCOPE

& ASTROLOGY

2025

Mystic Cat

Suite 41906, 3/2237 Gold Coast HWY

Mermaid Beach, Queensland, 4218

Australia

islandauthor@hotmail.com

Copyright © 2023 by Mystic Cat

Time set to Coordinated Universal Time Zone (UT±0)

All rights reserved. This book or any portion thereof may not be reproduced or used in any manner without the publisher's express written permission except for the use of brief quotations in a book review.

The information accessible from this book is for informational purposes only. None of the data should be regarded as a promise of benefits. It should not be considered a statutory warranty or a guarantee of results achievable.

Images are used under license from Fotosearch & Dreamstime.

Contents

January	16
February	24
March	32
April	40
May	48
June	56
July	64
August	72
September	80
October	88
November	96
December	104

Hello there, Let me explain why my horoscope books may give different readings for each zodiac sign. The sky is always bustling with astrological activity, and I want to focus on what's most important for each star sign.

Every zodiac sign is unique, and the planets up above affect them differently. When I create horoscopes, I pay extra attention to the most critical astrological events for a specific sign. Some days, there might be lots of stuff happening in the stars, but one thing stands out as the essential factor for a particular zodiac sign.

I also consider which planet rules a sign and its associated element. This in-depth consideration helps me tailor my interpretations to match a sign's characteristics.

Ultimately, my goal is to provide you with unique advice and insights that match the cosmic influences for your sign. By focusing on what makes each sign special, I hope to help you understand yourself better and navigate the energies around you. Embracing your sign's strengths and challenges is the key to making my horoscopes feel uniquely aligned for you.

Cosmic Blessings,

Sia Sands

ARIES 2025
HOROSCOPE & ASTROLOGY

Four Weeks Per Month

Week 1 – Days 1 - 7

Week 2 – Days 8 - 14

Week 3 – Days 15 - 21

Week 4 – Days 22 – Month-end

ARIES

Aries Dates: March 21st to April 19th

Zodiac Symbol: Ram

Element: Fire

Planet: Mars

House: First

Color: Red

Aries is the first astrological sign in the zodiac and is associated with the Fire element. People born under the Aries sign are known for their energetic, passionate, and dynamic nature. The ram, which is the symbol of Aries, embodies qualities of courage, leadership, and the drive to take action.

Aries individuals possess a strong sense of self and the ability to take initiative. They have a natural enthusiasm for life and a willingness to embrace new experiences and challenges. Ruled by Mars, the planet of action and energy, Aries individuals are known for their determination, assertiveness, and competitive spirit.

Aries is in the First House of the zodiac, associated with self-expression, personal identity, and new beginnings. This placement emphasizes Aries' focus on self-discovery and their desire to lead and make a mark on the world.

Red is often associated with Aries due to its connection to energy, passion, and vitality. This color represents the fiery and bold nature of Aries individuals.

In summary, Aries shows action, courage, and self-assuredness. Those born under this sign are often trailblazers and leaders, driven by their passion and desire to take on challenges head-on.

The Chinese Zodiac is a system that assigns an animal sign to each year in a 12-year cycle, and each animal is associated with certain personality traits and characteristics.

The Year of the Snake, in particular, holds special significance within Chinese culture and is rich in symbolism.

2025

The Chinese Year of the Snake

The Aries personality has a dynamic and enthusiastic nature. Aries individuals are known for their impulsive energy and desire to take action. They often approach challenges head-on and are driven by adventure and passion. However, when the Year of the Snake arrives, there could be a subtle shift in their approach.

During this year, Aries individuals delve into the Snake's inherent introspection and careful planning qualities. The Snake is known for its ability to patiently observe its surroundings before making a calculated move, which aligns with Aries' need to channel energy effectively.

The Year of the Snake encourages Aries to step back from their usual quick-paced approach and to take time for thoughtful consideration. It's a time for Aries to engage in strategic planning and evaluate their actions' long-term consequences. It doesn't mean that Aries should suppress their spontaneity, but rather that they should infuse it with a touch of reflection.

Aries' natural inclination towards self-discovery and self-expression could find harmony with the Snake's reflective nature. Aries might find themselves exploring their motivations, strengths, and weaknesses on a deeper level. This self-awareness could lead to more conscious decision-making and a greater understanding of how their actions impact themselves and those around them.

In relationships, the Year of the Snake could bring a heightened awareness of the intricacies of human interaction. Aries might take the time to understand the perspectives of others honestly and to communicate their intentions more clearly. This Snake year could lead to more harmonious connections and collaborations.

While Aries will always be known for their boldness and bravery, the Year of the Snake might help refine their approach. It's a year for growth through balance – combining their innate passion with the wisdom of careful consideration. By embracing the Snake's knowledge, Aries individuals could find new ways to achieve their goals while fostering personal growth and self-awareness.

ARIES 2025
HOROSCOPE & ASTROLOGY

JANUARY WEEK ONE

Get ready for some celestial vibes as the Moon rolls into Capricorn. The universe is giving you a cosmic nudge towards your career goals. You might suddenly feel that hustle is intensifying, and that urge to tackle those long-term plans is getting real. It's like the cosmos saying, "Hey, it's time to level up your ambitions and get serious about your grind." Whether chasing that promotion, launching your dream project, or hustling in your side gig, this lunar move is your sign to go to work.

But wait, because there's something extra special in the stars – a New Moon is coming! 🌑 This lunar event is like hitting the reset button for the universe. It's your chance to set fresh intentions, especially regarding your career path and how you want to show up. It's like getting a blank canvas to paint your dreams.

And then, the Moon glides into Aquarius. 🌙 That's when things get all quirky and independent. You're all about freedom and rebellion, ready to march to the beat of your drum. You're tuned into the cosmic frequency of innovation. You want to connect with your tribe and explore out-of-the-box ideas. ✦ ☾ ☽

JANUARY WEEK ONE

Get ready for a wave of romantic and dreamy vibes as Venus gracefully enters Pisces. This celestial dance brings an aura of enchantment to your love life and personal style.

Hold onto your cosmic seat belts because when Mars opposes Pluto, it's a powerhouse of intensity and transformation. It's like a cosmic showdown between the warrior and the underworld.

As the Moon gracefully moves into Pisces, your emotions take on a dreamy and intuitive quality. It's like a cosmic lullaby, encouraging introspection and a connection to the mystical realms.

When the Sun forms a harmonious sextile with Saturn, it's like a cosmic pat on the back for your hard work and dedication. This aspect brings stability and a sense of accomplishment.

Prepare for an energetic shift as the Moon charges into Aries. This cosmic spark ignites your passion and drive.

JANUARY WEEK TWO

☀ Mercury Ingress Capricorn: When Mercury dons its Capricorn attire, your thoughts take on a more practical and disciplined tone. It's like the cosmic accountant stepping in, urging you to organize your ideas and communicate with a structured approach.

☾ When the Moon gracefully glides into Gemini, your mind becomes a playground of curiosity and communication. It's like a cosmic invitation to explore new ideas and engage in lively conversations with those around you.

☾ As the Moon continues its celestial journey, entering Cancer, your emotions take center stage. It's as if the universe hands you a bouquet of feelings to nurture and protect, prompting you to seek comfort in the warmth of home and family.

◉ With Mars forming a harmonious trine with Neptune, your actions are guided by assertiveness and intuition. It's like a cosmic dance, where your desires align seamlessly with your dreams, allowing you to pursue your goals with grace and imagination.

JANUARY WEEK TWO

☉ When the Sun forms a harmonious trine with Uranus, expect a surge of innovative and liberating energy. It's akin to a cosmic breakthrough, inspiring you to embrace change and confidently express your individuality.

☽ The Full Moon graces the night sky, illuminating your path with its radiant glow. It's a culmination of energies, a cosmic spotlight on your achievements and emotions. Take this time to reflect and release what no longer serves you. Emotions run high as you stand in the moonlight's embrace.

☽ With the Moon's transition into Leo, your inner performer takes the stage. It's like a cosmic call to express your creativity and bask in the spotlight, unapologetically embracing your unique talents. Your heart radiates warmth, and you're ready for playfulness.

✦ But beware of cosmic clashes as Venus squares off with Jupiter. It's like a celestial debate between indulgence and restraint. While Jupiter tempts you with abundance, Venus reminds you to stay grounded and avoid overindulgence. Balance is the key.

JANUARY WEEK THREE

◌ When the Sun opposes Mars, it's like a cosmic clash between your willpower and actions. This aspect can bring about tension and impulsiveness. It's essential to balance assertiveness and restraint during this time.

◌ As the Moon gracefully enters analytical Virgo, you'll experience a shift towards practicality and attention to detail. This lunar influence encourages you to focus on organization and health-related matters, making it an excellent time for self-care routines.

⚡ The Sun's harmonious sextile with Neptune adds a touch of enchantment to your life. You'll find inspiration in your dreams and creative pursuits, and your intuition is heightened. It's like a cosmic daydream, inviting you to explore your imaginative side.

💜 Venus and Saturn align in conjunction, blending love with responsibility. This aspect encourages you to take a mature and practical relationship approach. It's a cosmic commitment where you can build lasting bonds based on trust and loyalty.

JANUARY WEEK THREE

🌙 As the Moon moves into charming Libra, your focus shifts towards partnerships and harmony. It's a cosmic reminder that relationships are a dance of give and take.

🗣 Mercury forms two harmonious sextiles, first with Saturn and then with Venus. These aspects enhance your communication skills and social interactions. You'll find it easier to express your thoughts with clarity and charm, making it an excellent time for negotiations and heartfelt conversations.

♒ As the Sun enters Aquarius, you'll feel a shift towards individuality and a desire for freedom. It's like a cosmic declaration of independence, inspiring you to embrace your unique qualities and connect with others.

🌑 The Sun's conjunction with Pluto intensifies your power and transformation. It's a cosmic rebirth where you can shed layers and emerge robust and self-aware.

🌙 As the Moon delves into passionate Scorpio, your emotions take on an intense tone. You'll crave authenticity and emotional connections, making it a time for soul-searching and exploring profound feelings.

JANUARY WEEK FOUR

❦ Mercury's trine with Uranus enhances your mental agility and innovative thinking. You'll find it easier to grasp new concepts and may even have brilliant flashes of insight. Your mind is like a cosmic lightning bolt, ready to strike with unconventional ideas.

☾ With the Moon's ingress into adventurous Sagittarius, your emotional landscape expands. You'll crave new experiences, exploration, and a broader perspective on life. It's a cosmic invitation to your inner wanderer.

♥ Venus's trine with Mars adds a touch of harmony to your relationships and passions. Your desires align with your affections, creating a harmonious flow.

☾ As the Moon moves into ambitious Capricorn, your focus shifts towards goals and responsibilities. You'll feel a strong desire for structure and achievement, making it an ideal time to tackle practical tasks.

☾ Venus's sextile with Uranus encourages you to embrace excitement and change in your relationships. It's a cosmic reminder that, sometimes, unpredictability can breathe new life into your connections.

JANUARY WEEK FOUR

Mercury's ingress into Aquarius marks a shift towards innovative thinking and a focus on community and group dynamics.

As the Moon enters Aquarius, your emotions are guided by a desire for freedom and individuality. You'll find solace in connecting with like-minded souls and pursuing unique interests.

Mercury's conjunction with Pluto ushers a profound period of deep thinking and transformation. Your mind dives into the depths of your psyche, uncovering hidden truths and empowering insights.

The New Moon marks a fresh beginning, like a cosmic blank canvas for your intentions. It's a potent time to set new goals and embrace the possibilities on your horizon.

Uranus turns direct, adding an electrifying energy to the cosmos. It's a cosmic gear shift for newfound clarity.

The Sun's trine with Jupiter brings optimism and abundance to your life. Your confidence soars, and you're open to opportunities for growth and expansion.

FEBRUARY WEEK ONE

💜 When Venus and Neptune align in conjunction, it's as if the cosmic romantics take center stage. Love, art, and beauty intertwine in a dreamy dance, inviting you to explore your deepest emotions and creative passions.

🌙 The Moon's ingress into fiery Aries ignites your inner warrior. Emotions run high, and you're ready to take on challenges boldly and enthusiastically. It's a time for courageous action and personal independence.

✻ Mercury's harmonious trine with Jupiter expands your mind and encourages optimistic thinking. Your thoughts are broadened, and you're drawn to intellectual pursuits and positive conversations. Your thoughts are infused with optimism and a thirst for knowledge, making it an excellent time for learning, planning, and open-minded discussions.

🌙 As the Moon moves into earthy Taurus, emotional well-being becomes a priority. You'll seek comfort, indulgence, and stability, making it an ideal time for relaxation and enjoying life's pleasures. You'll enjoy life's pleasures through delicious cuisine or the simple experience of being in nature.

FEBRUARY WEEK ONE

❦ Venus's transition into Aries ignites a passionate and assertive approach to love and relationships. You'll pursue your desires confidently and enthusiastically, embracing the thrill of the chase.

♃ Jupiter's direct motion signals a time of forward progress and growth in expansion, knowledge, and personal development.

☽ The Moon's ingress into communicative Gemini heightens your curiosity and desire for social connections. It's a great time for engaging in conversations, networking, and gathering information.

♥ Venus's sextile with Pluto adds depth and intensity to your relationships and desires. You'll experience a profound connection with others and may undergo transformative experiences in love and personal growth.

These cosmic influences create a tapestry of emotional depth, adventure, and expansion in your life, encouraging you to explore the mystical, embrace your passions, and welcome positive changes in your inner and outer worlds.

FEBRUARY WEEK TWO

☽ As the Moon gracefully moves into nurturing Cancer, your emotions take on a tender and compassionate quality. It's like a cosmic embrace that encourages you to prioritize home, family, and emotional well-being. During this time, you'll find solace in familiar surroundings and connections with loved ones.

◉ The Sun's conjunction with Mercury illuminates your mind with clarity and insight. It's as if a beam of intellectual light shines upon your thoughts, enhancing your communication skills and sharpening your mental faculties. This celestial pairing encourages meaningful conversations and precise expression of your ideas.

◉ Mars forming a trine with Saturn infuses your actions with discipline and determination. It's a cosmic alliance that empowers you to pursue your goals with focus and persistence. You'll find the endurance to overcome challenges and progress toward your ambitions.

☽ As the Moon ventures into charismatic Leo, you'll exude confidence and seek opportunities to shine. Your inner performer takes the stage, drawing you to creative and expressive pursuits.

FEBRUARY WEEK TWO

⚡ The Sun's square with Uranus brings an element of surprise and unpredictability to your life. It's like a cosmic lightning bolt that jolts you out of your comfort zone. During this period, be open to unexpected changes and opportunities for personal growth.

🌕 The Full Moon marks a culmination and a time of reflection. It's like a celestial spotlight that illuminates your achievements and long-term goals. Take a moment to celebrate your successes and consider any adjustments you want to make in your life's direction.

🌙 As the Moon moves into detail-oriented Virgo, your focus becomes practical matters and organization. You'll find satisfaction in tackling tasks precisely and paying attention to the finer details of life.

💜 On Valentine's Day, Mercury's ingress into compassionate Pisces adds a touch of romanticism to your communication style. It's as if your words are infused with empathy and sensitivity, making it an ideal time for heartfelt expressions of love and connection with your special someone.

FEBRUARY WEEK THREE

🌙 As the Moon gracefully glides into charming Libra, the cosmic spotlight is on harmony and balance in your emotional world. You'll find yourself naturally inclined to seek fairness and equilibrium in your interactions with others. It's a time when aesthetics hold particular appeal, and you might be drawn to beautiful surroundings that soothe your soul. During this lunar phase, cultivating peace and cooperation in your relationships takes precedence, making it an ideal moment to bridge differences and foster deeper connections.

🌙 As the Moon delves into the enigmatic waters of Scorpio, a profound shift occurs within your emotional landscape. Your feelings take on a deeper, more reflective quality akin to a cosmic invitation to explore the hidden realms of your psyche. During this phase, your intuition is heightened, guiding you toward a deeper understanding of your emotions and those of others. It's a transformative time when emotional authenticity becomes not just a choice but a necessity.

FEBRUARY WEEK THREE

The Moon's transition into adventurous Sagittarius stirs a sense of optimism and a thirst for exploration within you. Like a cosmic adventurer, you'll be drawn to new experiences and philosophical insights. The world becomes your classroom, and you'll relish the opportunity to expand your horizons through travel, education, or simply delving into new perspectives. This lunar phase amplifies your sense of freedom and urges you to seek personal growth and enlightenment.

Mercury's square with expansive Jupiter adds an enthusiastic and intellectually charged layer to your communication. Your ideas may take on grand proportions, and your conversations may overflow with optimism and idealism. While this cosmic aspect encourages visionary thinking, balancing your lofty dreams with practical considerations is crucial. Be mindful of overcommitting or making promises that might be challenging to fulfill. The key is to harness the power of your expansive thinking while remaining grounded and realistic in your plans.

FEBRUARY WEEK FOUR

☽ The Moon's graceful entry into the determined sign of Capricorn marks a time when your emotions become focused on structure, ambition, and practicality. You'll feel a strong need for order and organization, making it an ideal phase for setting goals and making long-term plans. During this lunar influence, you'll find satisfaction in tackling responsibilities and working diligently towards your aspirations.

● Mars, the planet of action and drive, turning direct heralds a significant shift in your energy and motivation. After introspection and reflection, you're ready to continue with renewed vigor and determination. Any obstacles or delays that may have slowed your progress in recent months are gradually lifting, empowering you to pursue your passions with increased enthusiasm.

☽ As the Moon progresses into open-minded Aquarius, your emotions take on a more progressive and humanitarian tone. You'll be drawn to innovative ideas, unconventional thinking, and social causes that align with your values. It's a time when your desire for freedom and individuality becomes pronounced, and you may find inspiration in the company of trailblazers.

FEBRUARY WEEK FOUR

◯ Mercury's conjunction with Saturn signifies a period of structured and focused thinking. Your mind becomes disciplined and detail-oriented, making it an excellent time for serious conversations, in-depth analysis, and strategic planning. This cosmic alignment encourages you to approach your responsibilities and commitments purposefully and clearly. Your words carry weight, and you can convey your ideas with precision and authority.

◯ Mercury's sextile with Uranus adds a dash of innovation and originality to your thinking and communication. Your mind is open to new ideas and unconventional solutions, and you're eager to explore uncharted territory intellectually. This cosmic connection encourages you to embrace change and spontaneity in your thought processes, allowing for exciting breakthroughs and creative problem-solving.

● The New Moon represents a fresh start and a blank canvas for setting intentions. It's time to plant the seeds of your desires. As the old cycle concludes and a new one begins, take a moment to reflect on your goals and aspirations and visualize the path ahead.

MARCH WEEK ONE

☽ When the Moon confidently charges into fiery Aries, your emotions receive dynamic and assertive energy. You'll feel an inner passion and the courage to tackle challenges head-on. It's a cosmic call to action, infusing you with the determination to initiate new projects.

☽ Venus, the planet of love and beauty, takes a moment to pause as it turns retrograde. During this introspective phase, you may reevaluate relationships and values. It's a period for reflecting on matters of the heart, reconnecting with past loves, or reconsidering your approach to beauty and aesthetics.

✹ Mercury's conjunction with Neptune marks a dreamy and imaginative period for your thoughts and communication. Your mind is receptive to creative and spiritual insights, and you may speak in poetic or metaphoric language. It's a time for exploring your intuition and embracing the mysteries of life.

⚡ The Sun's square with expansive Jupiter adds a touch of enthusiasm and optimism to your life. This cosmic alignment encourages you to balance aspirations with practical considerations and seek growth.

MARCH WEEK ONE

Mercury's transition into assertive Aries infuses your communication with boldness and directness. Your words carry a sense of urgency and independence, and you're unafraid to speak your mind. It's a time for taking the initiative and confidently expressing your ideas.

The Moon's entrance into grounded Taurus brings a sense of stability and a desire for comfort. You'll be drawn to the pleasures of life, from delicious meals to sensory experiences. Emotionally, you seek security and a peaceful environment.

Later, as the Moon transitions into Gemini, your mood is marked by a thirst for knowledge and social interaction. Your mind craves variety and stimulation, making it an ideal time for engaging in conversations, learning, and connecting with a diverse range of people.

Mercury's sextile with transformative Pluto adds depth and intensity to thoughts and communication. It's a cosmic invitation to delve fearlessly into profound subjects and engage in meaningful conversations. Your words have the power to transform, and you're drawn to explore the mysteries of life and human psychology.

MARCH WEEK TWO

☀ The harmonious trine between the Sun and Mars infuses your life with vitality and motivation. You'll feel a powerful drive to take action and make significant progress toward your goals. During this celestial alignment, your energy and assertiveness work hand in hand, allowing you to tackle challenges with confidence and determination.

🌙 As the Moon gracefully enters Leo, your emotions take on a vibrant and expressive quality. It's as if your inner performer steps into the spotlight, and you'll find joy in creative self-expression. Your heart longs for appreciation and recognition, making it an excellent time to share your talents and bask in the glow of admiration.

💬 Mercury's conjunction with Venus ushers in a period of sweet and harmonious communication. Your words are infused with charm and grace, making it easy to connect with others on a heartwarming level. This cosmic combination favors romantic conversations, creative collaborations, and expressions of affection. It's an ideal time for heartfelt conversations and expressing affection.

MARCH WEEK TWO

The Moon's transition into meticulous Virgo encourages a focus on practicality and details. You'll find satisfaction in organizing your life and addressing tasks with precision. This lunar phase is ideal for decluttering and fine-tuning your daily routines.

The Sun's conjunction with Saturn signifies a moment of disciplined focus and determination. Your sense of responsibility and commitment is heightened, making it an ideal time to set clear goals and work diligently toward them. This aspect brings a sense of stability and achievement, rewarding your hard work with tangible results.

The Full Moon illuminates your accomplishments and long-term goals. It's a time to celebrate your achievements and make adjustments to align your ambitions with your true desires. This phase encourages self-reflection and ensures your path forward is in harmony with your inner calling.

The Sun's sextile with Uranus adds a touch of excitement and innovation to your life. It may lead to unexpected changes or opportunities.

MARCH WEEK THREE

🔄 Mercury's retrograde journey initiates a period of reflection and review in your communication and thought processes. During this cosmic U-turn, you may find yourself revisiting old ideas, reconnecting with people from your past, and reevaluating your plans. Practicing patience and double-checking details in your conversations and decision-making is essential.

🌙 As the Moon delves into the intense waters of Scorpio, your emotions take on a profound and transformative quality. You're inclined to explore the depths of your feelings and uncover hidden truths. This lunar phase encourages introspection and a willingness to embrace vulnerability, leading to emotional growth and healing.

🌙 As the Moon transitions into adventurous Sagittarius, a sense of optimism and a quest for knowledge take center stage. You'll be drawn to explore new mental and physical horizons and seek to expand your horizons. This lunar phase fosters a love for freedom and a desire to embark on exciting journeys of self-discovery.

MARCH WEEK THREE

When the Sun forms a conjunction with dreamy Neptune, your connection to the mystical and artistic realms deepens. It's a time when your intuition is heightened, and you may find solace in creative and spiritual pursuits. Your dreams and ideals inspire you, and you're more attuned to the subtle energies that shape your reality.

The Sun's ingress into Aries marks the Vernal Equinox, a moment of balance and the beginning of a new astrological year. This transition brings a burst of energy and a sense of renewal. It's a time to embrace the spirit of leadership and initiative, set your intentions for the year ahead, and embrace the opportunities that come your way.

Venus's sextile with Pluto adds depth and intensity to your relationships and personal values. It's as if your connections take on a more profound and transformative quality. This cosmic alignment encourages you to explore your desires and build meaningful relationships. Whether in matters of the heart or your values, this aspect prompts you to dive deep and embrace authenticity.

MARCH WEEK FOUR

☽ When the Moon gracefully transitions into Capricorn, it ushers in a period of emotional grounding and dedication. During this lunar phase, your feelings take on a pragmatic and responsible tone, motivating you to focus on your long-term goals and commitments. You'll derive immense satisfaction from attending to your duties and nurturing your ambition, aligning your emotions with the pursuit of success and stability.

♣ The conjunction of the Sun and Venus casts a romantic and harmonious glow over your life as if the universe orchestrates a grand overture to love and beauty. In this celestial dance, your interactions brim with affection, and you'll be naturally drawn to express your adoration and indulge in life's finer pleasures. This period is an exquisite time to declare your feelings and revel in the magnificent tapestry of your relationships.

✦ The Sun's sextile with Pluto weaves a tapestry of depth and intensity into your experiences. This cosmic connection fuels a sense of transformation and empowerment, encouraging you to explore your innermost desires and embark on meaningful changes. During this time, you take steps toward personal growth.

MARCH WEEK FOUR

 Venus's sojourn into Pisces ushers in a season of romance and idealism. Your capacity for empathy and understanding deepens, enhancing your ability to forge emotional connections and experience spiritual bonding. Acts of kindness and selflessness take center stage, adding a touch of magic to your relationships.

 The conjunction of Venus and Neptune deepens the dreamy and romantic atmosphere. This period exudes creativity and yearning for transcendent love and beauty. Imagination takes flight, inspiring you to embrace artistic and spiritual pursuits and appreciate the ethereal aspects of existence.

 As the Moon steps into the fiery realm of Aries, a burst of energy and assertiveness infuses your emotions. This cosmic call to action encourages you to lead the way, face challenges head-on, and confidently express your desires.

 The arrival of the New Moon signifies a fresh beginning and an opportunity to set new intentions. This lunar phase invites you to envision the future you wish. It's a blank canvas where you can paint your dreams.

APRIL WEEK ONE

🏠 Transitioning into Cancer, the Moon focuses on emotional security and nurturing. Your heart seeks comfort and a sense of belonging. It's a time for cherishing family and creating a haven.

♎ Saturn's sextile with Uranus presents a harmonious cosmic dance between tradition and innovation. This aspect encourages you to embrace change while respecting existing structures. It's an excellent time to implement new and progressive ideas with a steady and thoughtful approach.

💧 Mars's sextile with Uranus sparks dynamic energy and the desire to break free from constraints. This alignment fuels your courage and compels you to take bold, decisive actions. Be prepared for a surge of independence and a thirst for excitement.

⛰ The trine between Mars and Saturn combines your drive and discipline, helping you tackle tasks with endurance and precision. It's a period where your ambitions align with your abilities, facilitating steady progress.

APRIL WEEK ONE

☺ As the Moon shifts into charismatic Leo, your emotions radiate with confidence and self-expression. You'll feel drawn to the spotlight and creative pursuits. It's a time to shine and showcase your unique talents.

🌞 The Sun's sextile with Jupiter illuminates your path with positivity and opportunities. This aspect invites good luck and a sense of expansion into your life. Your contagious optimism makes it easier to build rapport and achieve your goals.

💜 Venus's trine with Mars adds a touch of harmony and sensuality to your relationships. This alignment brings a balance between desire and affection. You'll find it easier to express your romantic feelings and connect passionately.

♣ Venus's conjunction with Saturn introduces a blend of love and commitment. During this period, your relationships take on a more serious tone. You're willing to invest time and effort in creating lasting bonds and finding beauty in the enduring aspects of love.

☿ Mercury's direct motion signals a turning point in communication as misunderstandings clear.

APRIL WEEK TWO

☾ Venus's sextile with Uranus sparks a cosmic connection that adds a touch of excitement and innovation to your love life and creative endeavors. It's as though the universe encourages you to infuse your relationships and artistic expressions with a dash of uniqueness and spontaneity. During this period, you'll enjoy the unexpected and may even explore unconventional forms of beauty and romance.

☾ As the Moon gracefully glides into Virgo, your emotions take on a practical and analytical tone. This lunar phase encourages you to pay attention to the details and strive for order and efficiency. You'll find solace in organizing your world and may be drawn to acts of service and self-improvement.

☾ Transitioning into Libra, the Moon casts a harmonious and diplomatic light on your emotions. This lunar phase encourages you to seek balance and harmony in your relationships and surroundings. You'll have a heightened appreciation for beauty and may feel a strong pull towards art, aesthetics, and social interactions.

APRIL WEEK TWO

🌕 The Full Moon marks a culmination, a cosmic spotlight on the seeds of intention you planted during the New Moon. It's a time for reaping what you've sown and celebrating your achievements. Emotions run high during this phase, giving it illumination and insight.

♀ Venus's direct motion signifies a shift from a period of introspection and review to one of forward momentum in matters of the heart and aesthetics. It's as though the cosmic artist is ready to paint her masterpiece with renewed inspiration. Relationships and artistic projects may now progress with greater clarity and purpose.

♏ With the Moon's ingress into Scorpio, your emotions take a more intense turn. It's as though you're peering beneath the surface of your feelings, seeking hidden truths and desires. This lunar phase encourages you to embrace transformation and explore the mysteries of life. Your emotions run deep, and you may find catharsis through self-exploration and letting go of the past. Find solace in this reflective energy as you explore the depths of your emotions.

APRIL WEEK THREE

🚀 Mercury's ingress into Aries adds a spark of enthusiasm and assertiveness to your communication style. This planetary transition ignites your mental agility, encouraging you to express your thoughts with boldness and courage. You'll find initiating conversations easier and taking swift action on your ideas.

🎨 When Mercury and Neptune conjoin, the boundaries between reality and imagination blur. This cosmic pairing enhances your intuition and creativity, making it an excellent time for artistic expression and spiritual exploration. Your dreams and intuitions are heightened, guiding you towards inspired ideas.

🦁 Mars's ingress into Leo infuses your actions with a generous dose of theatrical flair and charisma. You become more expressive and outgoing, eager to lead.

🌞 As the Sun moves into Taurus, your focus shifts towards stability, comfort, and the pleasures of life. This solar transition encourages you to connect with your senses and enjoy the simple, earthly delights. It's a time when you can savor the joys of the physical world.

APRIL WEEK THREE

☾ Mars's trine with Neptune blends your assertive energy with compassion and sensitivity. This harmonious connection encourages you to pursue your dreams with a sense of empathy and creativity.

✿ Easter Sunday brings an air of renewal and celebration. It's a time for spiritual reflection and connection with loved ones. The symbolism of Easter encourages you to embrace rebirth and transformation as you shed old patterns and welcome new beginnings.

♥ Venus's sextile with Uranus adds a touch of excitement and unpredictability to your relationships and social life. This harmonious connection may bring delightful surprises and opportunities for spontaneous connections. Your romantic and creative pursuits take on a unique and unconventional flavor.

✦ Mercury's sextile with Pluto signifies a profound dive into the depths of your thoughts and communications.

◊ When the Sun squares Mars, it's like a cosmic challenge that sparks a desire for action and assertion. This aspect can bring tension and assertiveness, encouraging you to overcome obstacles.

APRIL WEEK FOUR

☾ When the Moon gracefully moves into Pisces, your emotions take on a dreamy and compassionate quality. It's as if you're floating in the sea of imagination and empathy, making this an ideal time for artistic and spiritual pursuits. Your intuition is heightened, guiding you to deeper emotional connections.

● The Sun's square to Pluto intensifies your sense of power and transformation. This aspect may bring hidden issues to the surface, prompting a deeper examination of your desires and fears. It's a time for inner growth and understanding, even if it requires facing some uncomfortable truths.

♥ Venus's conjunction with Saturn grounds your relationships and values. This cosmic pairing encourages commitment and responsibility in matters of the heart. It's a time when you may take a more serious approach to love and appreciate the stability that enduring partnerships bring.

🔥 As the Moon enters Aries, emotions become more assertive and passionate. Being bold and courageous in your emotional expressions is a cosmic call to action.

APRIL WEEK FOUR

When Mars opposes Pluto, it's a cosmic clash of wills and power. This aspect can bring confrontations and power struggles, but it's also a time for profound transformation and regeneration. Your desires are intensified, and you may need to confront and release what no longer serves your growth.

As the Moon settles into Taurus, your emotions become grounded and focused on comfort and security. This lunar phase encourages you to indulge in life's pleasures and find serenity in the simplicity of existence.

The New Moon marks a fresh beginning, a chance to set new intentions and sow the seeds of your desires. It's a moment of introspection and planning where you can chart a course for the future. Take this opportunity to let go of the old and welcome the new.

With the Moon's move into communicative Gemini, your emotions are stimulated by curiosity and a need for social connection. It's when you're more inclined to engage in conversations, share ideas, and seek mental stimulation.

MAY WEEK ONE

☽ When the Moon enters Cancer, your emotions become deeply attuned to home and family. It's when you seek comfort and security, finding solace in the familiar and the nurturing. This lunar phase encourages you to connect with loved ones and create a sense of emotional well-being in your surroundings.

♥ The conjunction of Venus and Neptune creates an ethereal and romantic atmosphere in your love life and artistic expressions. It's as if the boundaries between reality and dreams blur, allowing for a profound and spiritual connection with your beloved. Your creative endeavors are infused with inspiration and a touch of otherworldly beauty during this aspect.

☀ As the Moon enters Leo, your emotions take on a regal and expressive quality. It's a time when you seek recognition, appreciation, and a stage to shine on. This lunar transit encourages you to embrace your inner performer and express your feelings with flair.

↺ Pluto's retrograde motion signifies a period of profound internal transformation. During this time, you're prompted to revisit and release old patterns.

MAY WEEK ONE

🗣 Mercury's sextile with Jupiter expands your communication and intellectual horizons. This harmonious aspect enhances your ability to express yourself with optimism and enthusiasm. It's an excellent time for learning, teaching, or sharing your ideas on a larger scale. Your conversations are filled with wisdom and a generous spirit.

☽ When the Moon moves into Virgo, your emotions become more analytical and service-oriented. It's when you find satisfaction in attending to details and improving efficiency. This lunar phase encourages you to organize and refine your life.

💜 Venus sextile Pluto deepens your emotional and romantic connections. This cosmic aspect brings intensity and a desire for profound relationship transformation. You're drawn to experiences that have a lasting impact, and your interactions are charged with passion and depth. This cosmic influence creates a time when your emotions are in harmony with your desire for depth and transformation in your relationships and creative expressions. You seek comfort and a profound connection with a touch of ethereal romance.

MAY WEEK TWO

❋ As the Moon gracefully enters Libra, you're immersed in an atmosphere of balance and harmony. Your emotions are attuned to the needs of others, and you seek fairness and peace in your interactions. This lunar phase encourages you to connect with loved ones, engage in diplomacy, and appreciate the beauty in your surroundings.

🌱 With Mercury's transition into Taurus, your communication style becomes more grounded and practical. Your words carry the weight of reliability and determination. You express your thoughts with patience and a touch of stubbornness, emphasizing the importance of stability and tangible results in your conversations.

🌘 When the Moon reaches Scorpio, your emotions delve into the depths of intensity and transformation. It's a time of heightened sensitivity and a desire to explore life's mysteries. This lunar phase encourages you to release what no longer serves you, embrace rebirth, and connect with the profound aspects of existence.

MAY WEEK TWO

🌕 The Full Moon, a culmination of the lunar cycle, illuminates your desires and achievements. It's a time to reap the rewards of your efforts and acknowledge your progress. Emotions run high, and you may gain insight into your path and intentions. It's a time for clarity and realization as the radiant Moon shines light on your desires and emotions.

🔍 Mercury's square with Pluto brings intense and transformative energy to your thoughts and communication. This aspect encourages deep research and the uncovering of hidden truths. Your words carry a weighty impact, but be mindful of power struggles in conversations.

♐ As the Moon transitions into Sagittarius, your emotions take on a more adventurous and optimistic tone. It's a time when you seek expansion, both mentally and physically. You're eager to explore new horizons, learn, and embrace different perspectives. This lunar phase encourages you to pursue your dreams and embrace the spirit of exploration.

MAY WEEK THREE

As the Moon gracefully enters Capricorn, your emotions take on a more grounded and practical tone. You're inclined to focus on your ambitions and long-term goals, seeking stability and structure. This lunar phase encourages discipline and a commitment to achieving your aspirations.

The conjunction of the Sun and Uranus brings an electrifying jolt of change and innovation. It's like the cosmos turns on a light switch, illuminating new possibilities and unconventional ideas. It encourages you to embrace your uniqueness and be open to sudden breakthroughs and revelations.

Mercury's square with Mars intensifies your thinking and communication, but it can also lead to impatience and impulsivity. Choosing your words carefully and avoiding hasty decisions or arguments during this time is essential. Harness the mental energy for productive and assertive discussions.

As the Moon moves into Aquarius, your emotions take on a humanitarian flair. This lunar phase encourages community involvement.

MAY WEEK THREE

☉ The Sun's sextile with Saturn brings a sense of discipline and responsibility to your endeavors. It's when you're more focused on long-term goals and willing to try to achieve them. This aspect encourages practical planning and the ability to work steadily toward your objectives.

☾ When the Moon gracefully enters Pisces, your emotions become dreamy and intuitive. You may be more in tune with your inner world and the mystical realms. This lunar phase encourages compassion, creativity, and a deeper connection to the emotions and experiences of others.

☀ The Sun's ingress into Gemini marks a shift in focus toward communication, learning, and versatility. You become more curious and adaptable, eager to explore various interests and engage in lively conversations. This solar transition encourages mental agility and a thirst for knowledge. Your interests diversify, and you become more mentally open. It's when you're eager to engage in lively conversations, learn new things, and connect with people.

MAY WEEK FOUR

💜 Venus's trine with Mars creates a harmonious dance between the feminine and masculine energies. Your relationships and passions are infused with a sense of balance and desire. It's when you can express affection and find harmony in your romantic connections.

☀ The Sun's sextile with Neptune brings a touch of enchantment to your life. Your intuition and creativity flow effortlessly, and you're more attuned to the spiritual and imaginative realms. This aspect encourages you to pursue your dreams and engage in activities that connect you with the ethereal.

💧 As the Moon charges into Aries, your emotions become infused with boldness and a pioneering spirit. You're ready to take action and assert your individuality. This lunar phase encourages you to enter the spotlight and lead enthusiastically.

⚹ The Sun's trine with Pluto marks a powerful and transformative energy. It's like a cosmic spotlight on your ability to create meaningful change and regeneration. It encourages you to tap into your inner strength and shift profoundly.

MAY WEEK FOUR

❦ Mercury's sextile with Saturn adds a practical and structured dimension to your thinking and communication. You're able to plan and express your ideas with precision and responsibility. This aspect supports disciplined and goal-oriented conversations.

● The New Moon marks a fresh beginning and an opportunity to set new intentions. It's like a cosmic reset button, allowing you to plant the seeds of your desires. This lunar phase encourages introspection, the formulation of new goals, and a sense of renewal.

🔍 Mercury's trine with Pluto intensifies your mental processes and communication. You're drawn to deep and transformative conversations, seeking to uncover hidden truths and profound insights. This aspect supports research, investigation, and understanding of complex subjects.

☼ The Sun's conjunction with Mercury illuminates your communication style and mental clarity. Your ideas and thoughts take center stage, and you can better express yourself confidently. This aspect encourages self-expression and effective communication.

JUNE WEEK ONE

♍ When the Moon gracefully moves into Virgo, your emotions take on a practical and analytical tone. This lunar phase encourages you to pay attention to the details and seek perfection in your daily life. You may find satisfaction in organizing, decluttering, and tending to your physical well-being. It's a time when you're inclined to be of service to others and seek out practical solutions to challenges.

♎ The Moon's shift into Libra brings a desire for balance and harmony in your emotional life. You become more focused on your relationships and social connections, seeking fairness and cooperation. This lunar phase encourages diplomacy and a sense of unity with those around you.

💜 Venus sextile Jupiter creates a harmonious blend of love and abundance. This aspect brings opportunities for expanding your social circle, enjoying the pleasures of life and deepening your connections with loved ones. It's a time when your heart is open to generosity and the joys of togetherness. This aspect encourages a generous and optimistic approach to matters of the heart and creativity.

JUNE WEEK ONE

🚀 Mercury sextile Mars ignites your mental processes and communication with dynamic energy. You're ready to express your ideas and take swift action. This aspect encourages assertiveness in your conversations and a proactive approach to problem-solving.

🌷 Venus's move into Taurus marks a time of sensual pleasure and a deeper connection with the physical world. You're inclined to appreciate the beauty of your surroundings and indulge in life's pleasures. This transit encourages you to savor the delights of the senses, whether through art, nature, or delightful cuisine.

🌑 As the Moon glides into Scorpio, your emotions take on an intense and transformative quality. You're drawn to explore the deeper layers of your psyche and may find yourself addressing matters of trust and emotional intimacy. This lunar phase encourages self-reflection, healing, and a connection with the mysteries of life. This lunar phase encourages self-discovery, delving into deeper dynamic layers, and seeking transformation. You may feel more in tune with your desires and inclined to explore hidden aspects of your psyche.

JUNE WEEK TWO

✳ Mercury's conjunction with Jupiter creates an expansive and optimistic mindset. Your thoughts and ideas infuse you with enthusiasm, and you feel open to learning and intellectual exploration. This aspect encourages broad thinking and a positive outlook.

☾ Mercury's move into Cancer brings a more emotionally sensitive and nurturing tone to your communication. You may find yourself expressing your thoughts and feelings with greater empathy and care. This transit encourages conversations that revolve around home, family, and personal matters.

☐ Mercury's square with Saturn introduces a touch of practicality and discipline to your thinking. It's a time when you may encounter challenges in communication, and it's essential to approach tasks and conversations with care and attention to detail.

▲ As the Moon enters Sagittarius, your emotions take on an adventurous and optimistic quality. You may feel a strong desire to explore new horizons and seek knowledge. This lunar phase encourages a sense of freedom and a thirst for new experiences.

JUNE WEEK TWO

Venus square Pluto stirs intense emotions in your relationships and desires. You may grapple with issues of control and power dynamics. This aspect encourages you to confront any underlying issues within your connections and transform them for the better.

Jupiter's ingress into Cancer marks a significant shift in the cosmic landscape. It's a time when expansion and growth are focused on nurturing and emotional connections. Jupiter in Cancer encourages you to explore opportunities related to home, family, and personal well-being.

The Full Moon illuminates the skies, marking a time of culmination and completion. It's a potent phase to bring ongoing projects to fruition and release what no longer serves you. This lunar phase encourages reflection and the celebration of achievements.

Mercury's sextile with Venus enhances your ability to express affection and appreciation. Your communication becomes more harmonious and pleasant, making it an excellent time for heartfelt conversations and connecting with loved ones.

JUNE WEEK THREE

⚡ Mars square Uranus brings a surge of rebellious and impulsive energy. It's like a cosmic lightning bolt that can lead to unexpected actions and a desire for freedom. While this aspect can be exciting, it also requires caution and awareness of impulsive behavior.

🪐 Jupiter square Saturn is a clash between expansion and restriction. It's like a cosmic tug-of-war between optimism and practicality. This aspect encourages you to find a balance between pursuing your dreams and meeting your responsibilities.

🌙 As the Moon gracefully enters Pisces, your emotions take on a dreamy and intuitive quality. It's like a cosmic lullaby, encouraging introspection and a connection to the mystical realms. This lunar phase fosters empathy and creativity, making it an ideal time for artistic pursuits and emotional healing.

⚔ Mars's ingress into Virgo marks a shift towards a more detail-oriented and analytical approach to action. You become more systematic in your endeavors, focusing on the nitty-gritty aspects of your projects. This transit encourages efficiency and careful planning.

JUNE WEEK THREE

🚀 As the Moon moves into Aries, your emotions take on a fiery and assertive quality. It's like a cosmic call to action, fueling your desire for independence and self-expression. This lunar phase inspires you to embrace challenges and initiate new ventures with enthusiasm.

☾ Jupiter square Neptune creates a clash between optimism and illusion. It's like a cosmic fog that can lead to misunderstandings and unrealistic expectations. This aspect encourages you to be cautious and discerning when pursuing your dreams and ideals.

🌷 As the Moon enters Taurus, your emotions adopt a sensual and grounded quality. This lunar phase encourages you to savor the beauty in simple indulgences, from delicious meals to the touch of luxurious fabrics against your skin.

☀ The Sun's ingress into Cancer marks the June Solstice, a time of celebrating the longest day of the year in the Northern Hemisphere and the beginning of summer. Cancer's energy brings a focus on family, home, and emotional connections, making it an ideal time for nurturing your closest relationships.

JUNE WEEK FOUR

🚀 Mars sextile Jupiter is a cosmic burst of energy and enthusiasm. It's like a rocket fueling your actions and endeavors with a sense of confidence and optimism. This aspect encourages you to take on challenges and expand your horizons, making it an excellent time for setting ambitious goals.

⌛ Sun square Saturn introduces a touch of challenge and responsibility. It's as if a cosmic taskmaster reminds you of your duties and commitments. This aspect encourages you to approach your responsibilities with determination, even if it feels like a roadblock.

☀ Sun conjunct Jupiter brings an air of optimism and opportunity. It's like a cosmic blessing, expanding your sense of abundance and luck. This aspect encourages you to embrace positive thinking and take advantage of opportunities that come your way.

🌑 The New Moon marks a fresh start and a moment for new intentions. It's like a cosmic blank canvas, inviting you to set new goals and make a fresh beginning. This lunar phase encourages you to plant the seeds of your desires and envision what you wish to manifest.

JUNE WEEK FOUR

Mercury sextile Uranus sparks inventive and unconventional thinking. It's like a cosmic light bulb moment, inspiring new ideas and a desire for intellectual exploration. This aspect encourages you to embrace innovation and open-minded communication.

Sun sextile Mars ignites your energy and drive. It's as if a cosmic fire energizes your actions and motivates you to take the lead. This aspect encourages assertiveness and a proactive approach to your goals.

Mercury's move into Leo infuses your communication with creativity. You'll express yourself with flair, as your ideas have a dramatic quality. This transit encourages self-expression and confidence.

Mercury trine Saturn adds stability and structure to your thinking. It helps you build solid plans and solutions. This aspect encourages careful consideration and the ability to focus on practical matters.

Mercury trine Neptune brings a touch of inspiration and intuition to your thoughts. It's like a cosmic muse guiding your creativity and enhancing your empathy.

JULY WEEK ONE

☾ As the Moon moves into Scorpio, it's like a cosmic dive into the mysteries of life and the realm of the subconscious. This lunar phase encourages self-reflection and exploring your innermost desires.

⚡ When Venus conjuncts Uranus, it's a cosmic rendezvous with excitement and change in your relationships and personal values. This aspect encourages you to embrace your individuality and be open to unexpected, liberating experiences in matters of the heart and finance.

❀ Venus's move into Gemini infuses your love life and social interactions with light and curious energy. It's like a cosmic butterfly, flitting from one delightful connection to another. This transit encourages versatility, playfulness, and a desire for mental stimulation in your relationships.

🌀 Neptune turning retrograde marks a time for introspection and reevaluation of your dreams and illusions. The cosmic fog lifts, allowing you to see clearly. This phase encourages discernment and a realistic approach to your spiritual and creative pursuits.

JULY WEEK ONE

💙 When Venus forms sextiles with both Saturn and Neptune, it's a harmonious dance between stability and enchantment in your relationships and artistic endeavors. These aspects encourage you to find a balance between the practical and the dreamy, making it a time for creative expression and lasting connections.

🔺 The Moon's ingress into Sagittarius brings a spirited and adventurous mood to your emotions. It's like a cosmic call to explore new horizons and embrace the unknown. This lunar phase encourages optimism, learning, and a sense of wanderlust.

✦ Uranus's move into Gemini sparks a shift in communication and thinking. It's like a cosmic lightning bolt electrifying your ideas and conversations. This transit encourages a fresh, innovative approach to information exchange and intellectual exploration.

💜 Venus trine Pluto deepens your connections and adds intensity to your passions. It's a cosmic key that unlocks profound emotional experiences. This aspect encourages transformative love and a deep sense of inner and outer beauty.

JULY WEEK TWO

🌑 When the Moon moves into Capricorn, your emotions take on a more serious and disciplined tone. It's like a cosmic mentor guiding you to approach life's challenges with a structured and pragmatic mindset. This lunar phase encourages you to set practical goals and work diligently toward your ambitions, even if it means temporarily setting aside more emotional matters.

🌝 The Full Moon is a decisive moment of culmination and release. It's like a cosmic spotlight illuminating the results of your efforts and intentions set during the previous New Moon. This phase encourages you to reflect on your achievements, celebrate your progress, and let go of what no longer serves your growth.

🌘 As the Moon enters Aquarius, your emotions take on a more innovative and open-minded quality. It's like a cosmic inventor sparking your curiosity and desire for freedom. This lunar phase encourages you to embrace your uniqueness and connect with like-minded individuals who share your visionary ideas.

JULY WEEK TWO

♄ Saturn turning retrograde marks a period of inner reflection and reassessment of your responsibilities and long-term goals. It's like a cosmic review of your life's structure and commitments. This retrograde encourages you to reevaluate your strategies, make necessary adjustments, and ensure your ambitions align with your authentic self.

☾ The Moon's ingress into Pisces brings a dreamy and empathetic influence to your emotions. It's as if a cosmic poet inspires your soul, fostering a deeper connection to your feelings and the world around you. This lunar phase encourages introspection, creative expression, and a heightened sensitivity to the emotional undercurrents in your life.

This week's cosmic events create a tapestry of emotions and self-discovery. You'll find a balance between practicality, celebration, innovation, inner contemplation, and emotional depth during this time. It's an opportunity to refine your path, express your unique qualities, and explore the depths of your inner world.

JULY WEEK THREE

☽ When the Moon enters Aries, your emotional landscape ignites with a burst of energy and initiative. It's like a cosmic call to action, urging you to embrace your adventurous side and take charge of your emotions. This lunar phase encourages you to pursue your desires with passion and enthusiasm.

☿ Mercury turning retrograde initiates a period of introspection and review in the realm of communication and thought. It's as if a cosmic messenger is asking you to pause and reflect on your ideas, words, and how you connect with others. This celestial event encourages you to revisit past conversations, clear up misunderstandings, and fine-tune your thinking.

☽ The Moon's ingress into Taurus brings a sense of stability and grounding to your emotions. It's like a cosmic anchor, helping you find comfort and security in the material world. This lunar placement encourages you to indulge in life's pleasures, connect with nature, and savor the sensory experiences that soothe your soul. It's a time for finding security and contentment in the tangible aspects of life.

JULY WEEK THREE

♥ Mercury sextile Venus creates a harmonious cosmic connection between your mind and heart. It's as if your thoughts and feelings dance in perfect sync. This aspect encourages sweet and meaningful communication, making it an ideal time for heartfelt conversations and expressions of love.

☽ As the Moon moves into Gemini, your emotions take on a curious and communicative flair. It's like a cosmic storyteller awakening within you, urging you to share your feelings and ideas with others. This lunar phase fosters intellectual curiosity and a desire to connect with people through engaging conversations.

This week, the celestial movements invite you to explore various facets of your emotional world, from fiery passion and introspection to grounded stability and harmonious communication. Embrace the dynamic energy of Aries, the reflective pause of Mercury retrograde, the sensual comfort of Taurus, the balanced connection between mind and heart, and the communicative spirit of Gemini. It's a journey of self-discovery and harmony with the world around you.

JULY WEEK FOUR

🦁 With the Sun's transition into Leo, you're stepping into a vibrant and self-assured phase. Leo, the zodiac's regal lion, brings with it an air of confidence and a desire to shine brightly. During this solar phase, you'll find that your inner performer is awakened, and you're encouraged to let your personality sparkle. It's a time to bask in the warmth of your radiant energy.

⚡ When the Sun forms a sextile with Uranus, you'll experience a delightful surge of innovative and unconventional energy. It's like a cosmic invitation to break free from the ordinary and infuse your life with excitement and unpredictability. This aspect encourages you to explore new horizons, experiment with fresh ideas, and embrace your individuality. Expect moments of inspiration and a willingness to embrace change.

💔 Venus square Mars ignites a dynamic and potentially passionate energy between the cosmic lovers. This square aspect stirs up desires and sparks like a cosmic romantic tango. While it can bring intensity to your relationships, it's also a reminder to find a balance between assertiveness and cooperation in matters of the heart.

JULY WEEK FOUR

● The arrival of the New Moon marks a fresh lunar cycle, like the beginning of a cosmic story. It's a time to set intentions and embark on new adventures. During this phase, you'll find that your emotions are in sync with your desires, and you're ready to plant the seeds of your future. Take a moment to reflect on your goals and aspirations, as the universe is prepared to support your journey.

✴ When the Sun opposes Pluto, it's like a cosmic tug of war between your ego and transformation. This intense aspect can bring power struggles to the surface, but it's also an opportunity for profound personal growth. You're encouraged to release what no longer serves you and embrace your inner strength.

▦ Venus's transition into Cancer adds a nurturing and emotionally attuned quality to your relationships and pleasures. This Venus placement encourages you to seek comfort and security in your connections. It's a time to express your affections through acts of care and compassion, creating a cozy and harmonious atmosphere in your personal life.

AUGUST WEEK ONE

💔 Venus square Saturn creates a challenging cosmic dance between love and responsibility. It's as if you're caught between the desire for romance and the need for structure. This aspect can bring about feelings of restriction and limitations in your relationships. It's essential to find a balance between your emotional needs and your commitments. By working through these challenges, you can strengthen your connections.

🌙 Venus square Neptune adds a touch of dreamy confusion to matters of the heart. It's like navigating through the fog of illusions and fantasies. This aspect can lead to misunderstandings or idealizing someone, which may not align with reality. Trust your intuition and take a practical approach to love, ensuring that your emotions are grounded in truth.

♐ With the Moon's ingress into Sagittarius, your emotions take on an adventurous and free-spirited quality. It's as if your heart yearns for exploration and new experiences. This lunar placement encourages you to embrace a broader perspective and seek out opportunities for growth and learning.

AUGUST WEEK ONE

🌑 As the Moon moves into Capricorn, a more grounded and practical emotional energy prevails. It's like a cosmic call to focus on your responsibilities and long-term goals. During this time, you may find satisfaction in accomplishing tasks and making progress in your professional life.

♎ Mars's ingress into Libra brings a sense of balance and diplomacy to your actions. It's as if a desire for harmony and fairness guides you. This cosmic shift encourages you to approach conflicts with a sense of grace and cooperation. Your efforts to create peace and maintain equilibrium are supported.

This week's astrological aspects create a complex interplay of emotions, responsibilities, dreams, and the pursuit of balance. While you may encounter challenges in your relationships and face moments of uncertainty, remember that each aspect holds the potential for growth and self-discovery. Embrace the adventurous spirit of Sagittarius, find practical solutions under Capricorn's influence, and navigate the delicate dance of love and responsibility.

AUGUST WEEK TWO

🚀 When Mars forms a trine with Uranus, it's as if the cosmic engines are firing on all cylinders. This harmonious aspect infuses you with a burst of energy, daring you to be bold and innovative in your actions. You'll find yourself drawn to new and exciting endeavors, unafraid to break free from routine.

⛔ However, Mars's opposition to Saturn introduces a contrasting force, creating a celestial tug of war between assertion and restriction. This aspect may present challenges and obstacles that test your patience and determination. You'll need to find a balance between your desire for independence and the need to adhere to rules and responsibilities. While this aspect can feel frustrating, it also provides an opportunity to build discipline and resilience.

🌕 The Full Moon is a culmination of energies, a celestial spotlight that shines on your accomplishments and emotions. During this phase, you'll experience a heightened sense of awareness and a need for closure. It's a time to reflect on your goals and the progress you've made. It's ideal to release what no longer serves you and celebrate your achievements.

AUGUST WEEK TWO

🜨 Mars's trine to Pluto heralds a powerful transformation. It's as if you're handed the keys to your inner powerhouse. This aspect empowers you to dig deep, confront your fears, and harness your inner strength. It's a time for pursuing your ambitions with unwavering determination. You can make profound changes and emerge from challenges more vital.

☿ Mercury turning direct is a cosmic green light. Communication, technology, and plans that may have felt stalled or tangled during its retrograde period now begin to flow more smoothly. You'll experience greater clarity and find it easier to make decisions and move forward.

♎ Saturn's sextile to Uranus brings a sense of balance to the clash of the old and the new. It's as if the cosmic architect and the innovator strike a harmonious chord. This aspect supports your efforts to build a bridge between tradition and progress. You can implement changes and reforms while respecting the stability of existing structures. It's a time for visionary ideas that can be brought into reality with patience and wisdom.

AUGUST WEEK THREE

✦ Mercury's harmonious sextile to Mars ignites a vibrant energy that can propel your actions and communication to new heights. This aspect creates a cosmic synergy between your thoughts and deeds, encouraging a dynamic, assertive approach to tackling challenges and pursuing your goals. During this period, your words carry impact, and your ability to express yourself with clarity and determination is enhanced. It's a promising time for not only formulating plans but also executing them with precision and enthusiasm. This cosmic alignment further fuels your problem-solving abilities, allowing you to navigate complex situations with finesse.

☽ As the Moon gracefully glides into Gemini, the cosmic atmosphere becomes a playground for your curiosity. You're drawn to the pursuit of knowledge, eager to explore new ideas, and open to diverse perspectives. This lunar influence nurtures your adaptability, making it an ideal moment for engaging in stimulating conversations, attending workshops, or delving into educational pursuits that expand your intellectual horizons.

AUGUST WEEK THREE

When the Moon makes its transition into Cancer, the emotional landscape takes center stage. This lunar placement heightens your sensitivity and empathy, encouraging you to connect deeply with your feelings and those of others. The nurturing qualities of Cancer bring a sense of warmth and compassion to your interactions, making it an opportune time to strengthen bonds with loved ones and address matters of the heart.

As the Moon continues its journey, entering the charismatic realm of Leo, a newfound sense of playfulness and self-expression permeates the cosmic tapestry. This lunar phase invites you to embrace your inner creative spirit and share your unique talents with the world. You'll find yourself naturally drawn to activities that allow you to shine in the spotlight. It's an ideal time to engage in artistic pursuits, celebrate your individuality, and infuse joy into your daily endeavors. This Leo lunar influence encourages you to let your inner child out to play and make the most of the creative opportunities that come your way.

AUGUST WEEK FOUR

☀ When the Sun enters meticulous Virgo, you might feel a shift towards a more organized and detail-oriented approach to life. Virgo's energy encourages you to pay attention to the finer points and embrace practicality. It's an ideal time for setting new routines, focusing on health and wellness, and getting your daily affairs in order. This solar influence guides you in refining your goals and taking a step-by-step approach to success.

🌑 With the arrival of the New Moon, you're presented with a cosmic clean slate. New Moons symbolize fresh beginnings and an opportunity to set intentions for the lunar month ahead. In Virgo, this New Moon emphasizes self-improvement, making it an excellent time for personal development, setting health-related goals, or reorganizing your life. What you initiate during this phase can grow over the coming weeks.

⚡ The Sun's square to Uranus adds an electric charge to the atmosphere. It's as if the universe is urging you to break free from routines and embrace change. While this aspect can bring unexpected developments, it also encourages innovation and a fresh perspective. Embrace the spirit of experimentation and be open to new ideas.

AUGUST WEEK FOUR

As Venus sashays into Leo, it brings an air of glamour and creativity to your relationships and personal style. Your love life may take on a more passionate tone, and you'll find enjoyment in artistic endeavors.

Venus forms a harmonious trine with Saturn, bringing stability and commitment to your relationships and creative pursuits. This aspect encourages lasting bonds and the cultivation of long-term goals in matters of the heart and personal expression. Your artistic endeavors may receive recognition, and your dedication to loved ones is evident.

Venus's trine to Neptune ushers in an aura of romance and compassion. You're more attuned to the emotional nuances of your relationships, making it an excellent time for deepening connections and expressing your affection. Creative and artistic pursuits also benefit from Neptune's dreamy influence.

Venus's opposition to Pluto can bring intense and transformative experiences in your relationships. Power struggles and hidden desires may surface, demanding an honest exploration of your feelings and needs.

SEPTEMBER WEEK ONE

🍂 As Saturn gracefully moves into Pisces, you'll experience a shift in the cosmic energies. Pisces, a water sign ruled by Neptune, is known for its dreamy and imaginative qualities. With Saturn's influence, you may find that your responsibilities take on a more compassionate and spiritual tone. It's a time to structure your dreams and connect with your intuition. This transit encourages you to find a sense of purpose in your creative and spiritual endeavors.

📖 Mercury's entrance into Virgo brings a strong emphasis on detail, analysis, and practicality in your thinking. You'll have a keen eye for precision and a desire to organize your thoughts and surroundings. It's an excellent time for problem-solving, communication, and getting your life in order.

⚡ When Mercury forms a square with Uranus, prepare for a surge of mental energy and a thirst for innovation. Your thoughts may come at lightning speed, and you could have brilliant insights. However, this aspect can also lead to restlessness and a desire to break free from routines. Embrace the unexpected and be open to unconventional ideas and solutions.

SEPTEMBER WEEK ONE

Mars square Jupiter creates a dynamic and ambitious energy. You'll be driven to take action and pursue your goals with enthusiasm. However, it's essential to watch for overconfidence or excessive risk-taking during this transit. Use your energy wisely and focus on well-thought-out plans to make the most of this dynamic aspect.

Uranus turning retrograde signifies a period of internal reflection and a review of your desire for change and independence. You may revisit past decisions and consider how they align with your current path. This retrograde phase encourages you to find more profound insights into your authentic self and the changes you seek.

The Full Moon marks a time of culmination and release. It's when the intentions you set during the New Moon come to fruition. Use this period to reflect on your achievements and let go of what no longer serves you. Emotions may run high, so be gentle with yourself and others. Embrace the lessons and experiences it brings, and use them to move forward on your journey.

SEPTEMBER WEEK TWO

☾ The Moon's entrance into Aries sets the emotional tone with a burst of fiery enthusiasm. You'll feel a surge of energy and a compelling desire to take the lead. It is the moment to initiate new projects, showcase your independence, and boldly pursue your aspirations. As impulsive as this lunar placement can be, it provides the drive to overcome obstacles and make a dynamic start.

☾ When the Moon moves into Taurus, a shift towards stability and practicality soothes the emotional landscape. Your focus turns towards seeking comfort and security, making it an ideal period to savor life's sensual pleasures. Financial matters come into sharper focus, and you may find satisfaction in creating a more stable and secure foundation for yourself.

☉ The Sun's harmonious sextile with Jupiter heralds a time of optimism and expanded horizons. This celestial alignment shines a spotlight on opportunities and encourages you to broaden your horizons, both mentally and physically. You're filled with a sense of confidence that propels you to set ambitious goals and embrace new adventures with enthusiasm. This aspect is akin to a celestial green light to head to your dreams.

SEPTEMBER WEEK TWO

As the Moon transitions into versatile Gemini, your curiosity and sociability come to the forefront. You'll find yourself eager to learn, connect with others, and engage in lively, intellectually stimulating conversations. This ingress time is a period where you'll want to expand your knowledge and engage with the world in a multifaceted way.

Mercury's sextile with Jupiter brings an extra layer of mental vitality and communicative finesse to your life. Your ability to express yourself and share your ideas is amplified. This aspect encourages positive thinking, planning, and taking a more comprehensive view of your life's circumstances. It's an auspicious time for educational pursuits, networking, and sharing your insights with a broader audience.

The conjunction of the Sun and Mercury signifies a period where your thoughts and self-expression are seamlessly aligned. Your intellectual faculties are sharpened, and your communication skills are at their peak. This alignment fosters mental clarity, making it a suitable time for essential conversations, negotiations, and articulating your ideas effectively.

SEPTEMBER WEEK THREE

🌙 The harmonious Venus sextile Mars aspect brings a delightful blend of passion and cooperation to your relationships and desires. It's a time when your connections with others can be both exciting and harmonious, allowing you to pursue your passions and work together effectively.

💬 However, as Mercury opposes Saturn, you might encounter mental challenges that require an organized and disciplined approach. It's a period when critical thinking and attention to detail are essential to overcome obstacles and make sound decisions.

☀ Mercury's entrance into Libra ushers in an era of balanced and diplomatic communication. Your interactions become more considerate, seeking harmony and fairness in discussions and negotiations.

🌊 Be cautious as Mercury opposes Neptune, as this aspect can bring confusion and miscommunication. It's vital to clarify your intentions and ensure you're on the same page with others to avoid misunderstandings.

SEPTEMBER WEEK THREE

🚀 Mercury's trines with Uranus and Pluto infuse your thinking with innovation and power. These aspects encourage inventive problem-solving and the ability to delve deeply into complex matters while finding unique solutions.

💚 Venus's move into Virgo triggers a shift in your love life and values, emphasizing practicality and attention to detail in your relationships. You may find beauty in the small, everyday gestures.

⚡ Venus square Uranus introduces an element of surprise and change in your relationships. Be prepared for unexpected shifts and a desire for more freedom and excitement in your personal life.

☿ The Sun's opposition to Saturn can bring feelings of restriction and responsibility. You might need to face challenges with patience and discipline during this phase.

● The New Moon marks a fresh start in your life. It's an excellent time for setting new intentions and launching projects.

SEPTEMBER WEEK FOUR

🔥 The arrival of Mars in Scorpio is akin to lighting a passionate fire in your life. Your determination and intensity are on full display as you wholeheartedly commit to your aspirations, unearthing your deepest desires in the process.

☀️ With the September Equinox, a season transition is marked, underlining themes of balance and change. This celestial event signifies the importance of recalibrating your life's equilibrium and considering the transformations necessary for your overall well-being.

♎ The Sun's entrance into Libra ushers in a period where harmony, relationships, and fairness take center stage. You're naturally inclined to restore equilibrium, especially within your connections, seeking to strike a balance between give and take.

🌊 Yet, the Sun's opposition with Neptune introduces an element of illusion or confusion into the mix. Navigating these waters calls for clarity in your interactions, ensuring you don't make decisions hastily or under the influence of deception.

SEPTEMBER WEEK FOUR

⚡ The Sun's trines with Uranus and Pluto infuse your life with a potent blend of transformation and innovation. You become more receptive to change, embracing opportunities for growth with open arms.

☽ The Moon's shift into Scorpio delves into the depths of your emotions, encouraging introspection and self-discovery. You'll find yourself exploring your innermost feelings and the driving forces behind your actions.

🗑 However, the square between Mars and Pluto can bring about intense power struggles and conflicts. It's crucial to approach such situations with a gentle touch, ensuring that you don't inadvertently intensify the dynamics at play.

🏔 As the Moon moves through Sagittarius, your emotions take on a more adventurous and expansive quality. You'll be drawn to explore new horizons, both intellectually and emotionally.

🏔 The Moon's subsequent entry into Capricorn shifts your focus to ambition and long-term objectives.

OCTOBER WEEK ONE

✺ As the Moon enters Aquarius, a sense of innovation and forward-thinking washes over you. This cosmic shift inspires you to embrace your uniqueness and explore new, uncharted territories. Your mind opens to fresh ideas and unconventional perspectives, encouraging you to break free from the ordinary and forge your path.

🐼 However, Mercury's square with Jupiter can lead to mental restlessness and a tendency to take on too much. While your enthusiasm knows no bounds, it's essential to maintain focus and prioritize your endeavors. Balance your creative ideas with practicality to make the most of this dynamic aspect.

☾ The Moon's transit into Pisces introduces an emotionally sensitive vibe to your life. You'll find yourself more attuned to the feelings of those around you and eager to lend a helping hand. This ingress is a time for empathy, selflessness, and heightened intuition. As the Moon moves into Pisces, you become more compassionate and intuitive. You're more attuned to the needs of others, making this an excellent time for acts of kindness and empathy. Dive into creative or spiritual activities to explore your inner world.

OCTOBER WEEK ONE

With the Moon's entry into Aries, your emotions gain a burst of fiery energy. You're ready to take action and pursue your goals with unwavering determination. During this cosmic phase, you feel more assertive and confident, making it an ideal time to initiate new projects or push forward with existing ones.

Mercury's entrance into Scorpio deepens your intellectual pursuits and adds a layer of intensity to your communications. Your mind delves into the profound and unearths hidden truths. You're not satisfied with surface-level explanations; you seek the underlying mysteries and uncover them with precision.

The Full Moon is a cosmic culmination, a time of closure, and a moment of revelation. It encourages you to release what no longer serves you and make space for new beginnings. It's a potent time for reflection, acknowledgment, and setting intentions for the future.

However, Mercury's square with Pluto can bring about intense and potentially confrontational communication. Seek clarity and avoid manipulative tactics to navigate this aspect successfully.

OCTOBER WEEK TWO

◐ Shifting into Gemini, the Moon heralds a more communicative and curious phase. Your mind becomes a fertile ground for ideas, and the desire for lively conversations and intellectual exploration takes center stage. Engage in discussions, express your thoughts, and let the free flow of ideas stimulate your mental faculties. It's a cosmic invitation to embrace the power of communication and expand your mental horizons.

◐ Venus, now in Libra, finds itself in a cosmic dance of opposition with stern Saturn. This celestial tango introduces a note of tension into matters of love and aesthetics. Balancing your desires with practical considerations becomes crucial. Patience and diplomacy are your cosmic allies during this time as you navigate the delicate dance between passion and responsibility.

◐ As the Moon transitions into Cancer, emotions swell, and a nurturing energy prevails. It's a time to seek solace in the comfort of home and close relationships. Allow yourself to be attuned to your feelings and those of others, fostering a sense of security and emotional well-being. The cosmic currents encourage you to create a safe and loving space, both within and around you.

OCTOBER WEEK TWO

💔 Venus, now gracing Libra, adds a touch of elegance and charm to your interactions. However, an opposition with dreamy Neptune introduces an element of ambiguity. Be cautious of idealizing situations or people, and strive for clarity in matters of the heart. The cosmic advice is to blend romance with a discerning eye, finding the balance between fantasy and reality.

🔄 Pluto's direct motion signals a shift in the cosmic currents. It's as if the universe is urging you to embrace transformation and release any lingering shadows.

🌙 The Moon's entrance into Leo infuses the atmosphere with a radiant and theatrical flair. You're encouraged to bask in the spotlight of creativity and self-assurance. The cosmic stage is set for you to shine, allowing your unique brilliance to illuminate the world around you.

🌙 Venus, in a harmonious trine with innovative Uranus, invites a sprinkle of excitement into your love life and creative endeavors. Embrace spontaneity and be open to unconventional expressions of affection. The cosmic message is clear: Infuse relationships with a touch of unpredictability and let your creativity soar. 🌙💚✨

OCTOBER WEEK THREE

☽ As the Moon gracefully moves into Virgo, an energy of meticulous attention and practicality permeates the cosmic atmosphere. You find comfort in organizing your surroundings and streamlining daily routines. This lunar phase encourages you to attend to the finer details, fostering a sense of order and efficiency in your endeavors.

☀ The celestial stage is set for a cosmic showdown as the Sun squares off with expansive Jupiter. This clash creates an atmosphere of tension between your desire for personal expression and the need for measured growth. Balancing confidence with humility becomes the key to navigating this cosmic terrain.

☽ Transitioning into Libra, the Moon beckons you into the realm of harmonious connections and aesthetic appreciation. It's a time when your focus shifts to partnerships and the beauty that exists in balanced interactions. Engage in conversations that promote understanding and seek out the beauty in both yourself and others.

OCTOBER WEEK THREE

◪ Mercury and Mars engage in a celestial dance, aligning in a conjunction that sparks a dynamic interplay between thought and action. Your mental agility is heightened, and there's a drive to articulate your ideas with assertiveness. Use this energy to communicate your intentions clearly and passionately.

● The New Moon graces the cosmic stage, signaling a potent moment for fresh beginnings. This lunar phase invites you to set intentions, plant seeds of growth, and embrace the potential for transformation. It's a cosmic blank canvas, and the energies support your endeavors to initiate new chapters in various aspects of your life.

● As the Moon slips into Scorpio, emotions deepen, and there's an inclination to explore the mysteries that lie beneath the surface. This lunar phase encourages you to delve into the realms of introspection and self-discovery, unearthing hidden truths and embracing the transformative power of vulnerability.

In this cosmic journey, the Moon's movements guide you through phases of practicality, harmonious connections, and the initiation of new beginnings. ☽ ☾ ✦

OCTOBER WEEK FOUR

☾ Neptune's ethereal ingress into Pisces bathes the cosmos in a dreamy and intuitive energy. This watery alignment enhances your creativity, compassion, and spiritual connection. Dive into the realms of imagination and let your intuition guide you as you navigate the currents of life.

☉ As the Sun gracefully enters Scorpio, the cosmic spotlight turns toward themes of transformation and regeneration. This solar influence encourages you to delve deep into the mysteries of your psyche, uncovering hidden truths and embracing the power of renewal.

● The square between the Sun and transformative Pluto brings a dynamic interplay of energies. This celestial tension invites you to confront power dynamics and seek personal empowerment. Embrace the opportunity for rebirth and regeneration, letting go of what no longer serves your higher purpose.

✷ Mercury's harmonious trine with expansive Jupiter creates a cosmic bridge between intellect and wisdom. It's a favorable time for learning, sharing ideas, and seeking a broader understanding of the world.

OCTOBER WEEK FOUR

🚀 Mars' trine with expansive Jupiter brings a surge of energy and enthusiasm. This dynamic alignment propels your actions forward with confidence and vitality. It's a time to pursue your goals with enthusiasm, embracing opportunities for growth and expansion.

☿ Mercury's ingress into adventurous Sagittarius amplifies the spirit of exploration and learning. Your mind seeks higher knowledge and broader perspectives. Embrace the thrill of discovery and engage in intellectual pursuits that expand your horizons.

⚙ Mars' trine with grounded Saturn provides a harmonious blend of energy and discipline. This cosmic alliance supports you in taking strategic and well-planned actions. It's a time to build on your ambitions with a steady and focused approach.

⚡ Mercury's opposition to Uranus introduces an element of unpredictability to your thoughts and communication. Embrace the unexpected, and be open to innovative ideas and perspectives. Flexibility in thinking can lead to breakthroughs and insights.

NOVEMBER WEEK ONE

☽ As the Moon charges into Aries, a surge of energy and enthusiasm propels you forward. Embrace this dynamic and assertive lunar energy to kickstart new initiatives and take bold strides toward your goals. It's time to trust your instincts and initiate action.

♎ Venus square Jupiter introduces a cosmic dance between love and expansion. While Venus seeks harmony and connection, Jupiter encourages abundance and growth. Navigate the balance between indulgence and moderation in relationships, and be mindful of overextending your resources.

♂ Mars trine Neptune infuses your actions with a touch of magic and inspiration. Your drive is guided by intuition and creativity, allowing you to pursue your goals with a sense of purpose and spiritual insight. Trust the flow and let your imagination guide your actions.

♐ Mars' ingress into Sagittarius sets the stage for dynamic and adventurous energy. Your pursuits gain momentum as the enthusiastic influence of Sagittarius ignites your passions. Embrace a spirit of exploration and take courageous strides toward your ambitions.

NOVEMBER WEEK ONE

⚡ Mars opposed Uranus sparks an electric and unpredictable energy. Be prepared for sudden changes, unexpected events, and a call for freedom. Embrace flexibility and stay open-minded as you navigate the dynamic shifts in your path.

🌕 The Full Moon illuminates the sky, casting light on your achievements and revealing the culmination of efforts. Reflect on your journey, celebrate accomplishments, and release what no longer serves.

⛰ Mars sextile Pluto brings a powerful alignment of energy. Your actions are fueled by deep determination and resilience. Use this intense combination to overcome challenges and drive transformation in your endeavors.

🌐 The Moon's ingress into Gemini lightens the cosmic mood, encouraging curiosity and communication. It's a favorable time for social connections, intellectual pursuits, and engaging in light-hearted conversations.

🦂 Venus' ingress into Scorpio adds depth and intensity to matters of the heart. Relationships may enter a more profound and transformative phase. Embrace authenticity and the emotional depths of connections.

NOVEMBER WEEK TWO

🌀 Brace yourself for a celestial spectacle as Uranus, the harbinger of innovation, steps into the grounded realm of Taurus. This cosmic rendezvous signals a seismic shift, challenging the status quo in matters of stability and security. It beckons you to embrace unpredictability, infusing your life with revolutionary ideas and transformative energies. Get ready to navigate uncharted waters and welcome the winds of change.

💔 As Venus locks horns with Pluto in a cosmic clash, the stage is set for a profound metamorphosis in your relationships. This intense interplay delves into the depths of emotional landscapes, urging you to confront hidden shadows and navigate the terrain of rebirth in matters of the heart. It's a cosmic crucible for growth and transformation.

🌙 The lunar energies take center stage as the Moon gracefully pirouettes into Cancer. Emotions swell like the tides, inviting you to explore the intimate shores of your inner world. This nurturing energy encourages self-care, fostering a connection with your intuitive depths. Find solace in the comforts of home and the warm embrace of loved ones during this cosmic embrace.

NOVEMBER WEEK TWO

🔄 Mercury, the cosmic messenger, takes a reflective pause in its retrograde dance. This celestial backspin encourages you to review, reassess, and realign. It's a cosmic pitstop, prompting a closer look at unresolved matters, making it a favorable time for introspection and refining your path forward.

🦁 The lunar spotlight now shines on Leo, infusing the cosmic tapestry with radiant creativity and self-expression. This phase is a call to step into the limelight of your authenticity, unleashing the inner performer. Engage in activities that bring joy and playfulness.

🔍 Jupiter, the expansive giant, takes a reflective turn as it starts its retrograde journey. This cosmic realignment invites a review of personal beliefs, philosophies, and growth trajectories. It's a celestial sabbatical, urging inner exploration and refining your vision for the future.

💨 Mercury's dynamic conjunction with Mars adds a burst of energy to communication and mental agility. Seize this potent alignment to express thoughts assertively, tackle tasks with precision, and overcome challenges.

NOVEMBER WEEK THREE

✨ Bask in the expansive energy as the Sun forms harmonious trines with both Jupiter and Saturn. This cosmic alliance bestows a sense of balance and optimism, amplifying your ability to manifest your aspirations with discipline and wisdom. It's a celestial green light, encouraging you to reach for your dreams while staying grounded in practicality.

💬 Mercury, the cosmic messenger, weaves a dynamic dance in the cosmic tapestry. Its sextile with Pluto intensifies communication, fostering deep insights and the potential for transformative conversations. As Mercury voyages into Scorpio, the heavenly waters deepen, urging you to explore profound truths and hidden realms of thought.

⚡ Brace yourself for the unexpected as Mercury opposes Uranus. This cosmic alignment may bring surprising revelations, sudden shifts in perspective, or electrifying ideas. Embrace the spontaneity and be open to innovative solutions that arise during this period of mental stimulation.

NOVEMBER WEEK THREE

● The New Moon marks a cosmic reset, a moment to plant the seeds of intention for the upcoming lunar cycle. Set your aspirations and desires with clarity, allowing the cosmic energies to support the germination of new beginnings in your life.

○ The Sun joins forces with Mercury in Sagittarius, infusing the atmosphere with a spirit of adventure and a thirst for knowledge. This cosmic duo encourages you to broaden your horizons, explore new perspectives, and embark on intellectual journeys that expand your understanding of the world.

🌠 Uranus and Neptune engage in a harmonious sextile, fostering a blend of innovation and inspiration. This cosmic collaboration invites you to explore inventive ideas with a touch of divine guidance. Be open to the unexpected and trust the cosmic currents to lead you toward new and exciting horizons.

☌ However, be prepared for a celestial tug-of-war as the Sun opposes Uranus. This cosmic clash may bring about unexpected disruptions, challenging your desire for stability. Stay flexible and pave the way for change.

NOVEMBER WEEK FOUR

☀ As the Sun joyfully enters Sagittarius, a burst of adventurous energy envelops your essence. It's like the universe hands you a map and encourages you to explore the vast landscapes of knowledge and experience. Sagittarius' influence infuses your spirit with optimism and a thirst for wisdom. Embrace the freedom to broaden your horizons, engage in new pursuits, and let the fires of enthusiasm guide your journey. This solar transit sparks a radiant flame within, urging you to seek the truth and expand your consciousness.

🌐 The alignment of Mercury and Jupiter in a trine creates a cosmic bridge between intellect and expansion. Your thoughts take flight, soaring to new heights of optimism and broad-mindedness. This celestial collaboration enhances your ability to see the bigger picture, facilitating successful communication and the pursuit of knowledge. Embrace the spirit of growth and intellectual exploration during this harmonious transit.

☀ The harmonious sextile between the Sun and Pluto empowers you with a profound sense of personal transformation. It's a cosmic nudge encouraging you to delve into the depths of your inner power.

NOVEMBER WEEK FOUR

♄ As Saturn, the cosmic taskmaster, turns direct, a sense of forward momentum and clarity permeates your endeavors. Delays and obstacles begin to dissipate, and the lessons learned during Saturn's retrograde period become the building blocks for your future success. It's a time to apply the wisdom gained, embrace responsibilities, and move steadily toward your long-term goals.

☿ With Mercury resuming its direct motion, the cosmic communication channels open up, and clarity prevails. Delays and misunderstandings begin to dissipate, allowing you to move forward with plans and projects. It's a time for clear thinking, effective communication, and implementing the insights gained during Mercury's retrograde phase.

♀ The opposition between Venus and Uranus creates a dynamic tension in matters of love and aesthetics. Expect the unexpected in relationships and creative pursuits. This celestial dance encourages you to break free from routine and explore unconventional expressions of beauty and spontaneity in romance.

DECEMBER WEEK ONE

☽ The Taurus moon brings a sense of grounded serenity to your emotional landscape. Like a gentle touch of nature, this cosmic influence encourages you to find stability and comfort in your feelings. Embrace the earthy energy, allowing yourself to savor the simple pleasures and cultivate a sense of security in your emotional world.

♥ Experience a cosmic dance as Venus sextiles Pluto, infusing your relationships with transformative energy. Dive into the depths of passion and connection, allowing the power of love to create positive changes. This celestial alignment invites you to explore the profound and intense aspects of your relationships with others.

☽ The moon gracefully enters Gemini, ushering in a dynamic and curious energy. Your emotions take on a light and adaptable quality, prompting a desire for variety and mental stimulation. Embrace the social and communicative vibe of Gemini, fostering connections and exploring diverse perspectives.

DECEMBER WEEK ONE

🌕 The full moon graces the night sky, illuminating emotions and bringing things to fruition. This decisive lunar phase is a culmination of energy, signaling a time to reflect on achievements and release what no longer serves you. Embrace the heightened emotions and use the full moon's energy for clarity and manifestation.

🌙 Transition into Cancer's nurturing embrace as the moon moves into this sensitive and intuitive sign—your emotional focus shifts toward home, family, and a desire for emotional security.

🌑 Dive into the mystical realms as Mercury trines Neptune, enhancing your intuitive and imaginative faculties. This cosmic connection opens the door to creative expression, spiritual insights, and compassionate communication. Allow your mind to dance in the realms of inspiration and embrace the poetic flow of thoughts.

🌙 The moon enters Leo, bringing a burst of vibrant and expressive energy to your emotional state. Like a cosmic performer, Leo encourages you to shine and express yourself with confidence.

DECEMBER WEEK TWO

◊ Feel the cosmic tension as Mars squares Saturn, stirring the arena of action and discipline. Challenges may arise, testing your resolve. Stand firm in the face of adversity, channeling Mars' fiery energy with Saturn's strategic wisdom. It's a time for measured steps and deliberate actions as you navigate this celestial square.

☽ The Moon gracefully glides into meticulous Virgo, guiding your emotions toward a space of practicality and attention to detail. Find solace in the beauty of order and the satisfaction of well-executed plans. Embrace the lunar energy as it encourages an organized approach to your emotional landscape.

☾ Neptune turns direct, releasing a mystical current into the cosmic waters. Dreams awaken, and illusions dissipate as Neptune resumes its forward motion. It's a time to reconnect with the ethereal realms and trust the flow of cosmic energies.

⚡ Brace yourself for the dynamic dance of Mercury opposing Uranus, creating sparks of intellectual electricity. Unpredictability colors your thoughts, and innovative ideas take center stage.

DECEMBER WEEK TWO

♐ Mercury gracefully enters Sagittarius, adding a touch of adventurous flair to your thoughts and expressions. Your mind seeks expansive horizons, and your words take flight like arrows aiming for the stars. Embrace the spirit of exploration and let the cosmic archer guide your intellect toward new and exciting possibilities.

☽ The Moon enters diplomatic Libra, infusing the cosmic stage with a sense of harmony and balance. Emotions find equilibrium, and relationships take center stage. Seek the beauty in connections, and let the cosmic scales of Libra guide you towards understanding and cooperation in your emotional interactions.

✦ Mercury sextiles Pluto, creating a cosmic synergy between intellect and transformation. Your words hold a potent allure, and your thoughts delve into the depths of profound insights. Explore the transformative power of communication during this celestial alignment.

◉ Mars squares Neptune, creating a celestial tango between action and illusion. Navigate the cosmic dance with caution, as the fog of uncertainty may cloud your energetic pursuits.

DECEMBER WEEK THREE

◐ Mars, the fiery warrior, strides into disciplined Capricorn, infusing your actions with ambition and strategic intent. Your drive takes on a focused and determined quality, propelling you toward your goals. Channel the energy of Mars in Capricorn for resilient perseverance and methodical progress on your cosmic journey.

◯ The Sun squares Saturn, creating a cosmic challenge that calls for patience and perseverance. Obstacles may arise, testing your resolve. Approach challenges with a steady heart and a commitment to your goals. The celestial square encourages you to build resilience and face difficulties with determined strength.

☾ Sagittarius beckons as the Moon dances into this adventurous sign. Embrace the expansive energy of Sagittarius, and let your emotions soar into the vast horizons of possibilities. It's a time to seek inspiration, explore new perspectives, and embrace the joy of discovery on your emotional journey.

DECEMBER WEEK THREE

🌑 The cosmic canvas is reset with the arrival of the New Moon, a celestial invitation to set intentions and plant seeds of growth. Harness the energy of the New Moon in Sagittarius to envision new horizons and embark on fresh adventures. Embrace the cosmic reset button, and let your intentions bloom with the promise of the lunar cycle.

🌒 Capricorn takes center stage as the Moon steps into this earthy realm, grounding emotions in practicality and ambition. Channel the lunar influence to focus on long-term goals and embrace a disciplined approach to your emotional landscape. Capricorn's energy encourages you to climb the cosmic mountain with determination.

🌚 The enigmatic Black Moon joins the cosmic dance in Sagittarius, bringing an air of mystery and depth to your emotional landscape. Embrace the subtle currents of the Black Moon's energy as it whispers ancient wisdom and stirs the depths of your intuition. Allow its influence to guide you on a journey of inner exploration.

DECEMBER WEEK FOUR

💜 Venus squares Neptune, creating a cosmic dance between love and dreams. Embrace the ethereal beauty of this celestial square, but be mindful of illusions that may color matters of the heart. Ground your romantic ideals in reality and navigate the waves of emotions with sensitivity and clarity.

✹ Venus gracefully enters Capricorn, adding a touch of practicality to matters of love and pleasure. Your approach to relationships becomes more grounded, and you may find satisfaction in building stable foundations. Embrace commitment and responsibility in matters of the heart as Venus dances through the earthy sign of Capricorn.

☾ The cosmic tides carry the Moon into dreamy Pisces. Embrace the poetic and intuitive energy of Pisces as your emotions flow like a gentle stream. Dive into the realm of imagination and creativity, allowing your feelings to meander through the cosmic currents of this watery sign.

DECEMBER WEEK FOUR

🌙 A burst of fiery energy emerges as the Moon enters Aries, igniting your emotional landscape with passion and enthusiasm. Embrace the spirit of initiative and be open to exciting possibilities. Your emotions become a dynamic force propelling you toward new adventures and experiences.

🌙 The Moon gracefully glides into Taurus, grounding the cosmic energy in earthly sensibility. Embrace the stability and pleasure-seeking qualities of Taurus as your emotions settle into a tranquil rhythm. It's a time to indulge in sensory delights and find comfort in the simple joys that surround you.

▨ Mercury squares Saturn, creating a celestial tension between communication and structure. Be mindful of potential challenges in expressing your thoughts and ideas. Use this cosmic square as an opportunity to strengthen your mental discipline and approach communication with clarity and precision.

🌙 The Moon enters communicative Gemini, inviting a breeze of intellectual curiosity into your emotional landscape.

NOTES

NOTES

NOTES

Astrology, Tarot & Horoscope Books.

Mystic Cat

www.ingramcontent.com/pod-product-compliance
Lightning Source LLC
LaVergne TN
LVHW051844080426
835512LV00018B/3055